My Quotes to the Buyer of my First Book

"The inspiration and the foresight you obtain from my book are packed with energy."

"Put a positive view on ALL of my quotes, phrases, statements and poetry and your journey will be enriched."

"My philosophical view on life runs deeper than the ocean floor, and we will never know how deep that may be. Wow, that's deep."

"We fear failure when we look up."

"Don't do all of it, do some of it and all will have to wait."

"A baseball laugh: If the pitcher keeps throwing the ball across the plate and you don't swing, I will bet you that the ball will not hit itself."

Making a way for everyone today is the essential ingredient to helping others.

The Spirit of Number Four

A Book of Quotes, Statements, Phrases and Poetry

by

Keith Davis

Never allow a day to go by that you do not recognize how important you are to the world.

authorHOUSE®

AuthorHouse™
1663 Liberty Drive
Bloomington, IN 47403
www.authorhouse.com
Phone: 1 (800) 839-8640

Published by AuthorHouse   03/21/2017

ISBN: 978-1-5246-4770-4 (sc)
ISBN: 978-1-5246-4769-8 (e)

Library of Congress Control Number: 2016917995

Print information available on the last page.

This book is printed on acid-free paper.

This book is dedicated to my son Keith W. Davis. May this book give you wisdom, knowledge, creative thoughts that will guide you through your journey in life.

Foreword by Kelcy Williams
Playwright/Screenwriter & Director
Flint Township, Michigan

*The book, **The Spirit of Number 4,** by Keith Davis gives the readers insight into the mind of a man who has experienced life to its fullest. The Author expresses quotes that have helped him to become successful over the years and will help readers become successful as well. One of my favorite quotes "you can't stop me from being great" is a quote that every reader young and old should adapt in their lives. If you believe others can stop you from being* great, then you will always allow people to keep you from your destiny.

Personally knowing the Author and being totally aware of the success he has accomplished, validates the content in his book. "When faced with obstacles, the creative side finds a way around whatever it takes to continue to pursue excellence". This is the life of the Author. He not only quoted this statement but he lives it. Keith was raised in the streets of Detroit, Michigan and with barely any money in his pocket took a chance years ago and moved to San Diego. With all odds against him and no one to depend on, he made it. This saying is very true and Keith lives up to this statement each and every day.

One other quote that I personally know fits the Author very well is "give and keep giving until it becomes a habit". When I read that all I could say was wow! Keith has given not just his money, his time, or his wisdom, but he has constantly given of himself. I know this first hand and if the readers of this book take *on this mentality, they will too find success in giving. Keith believes in encouraging young people to become successful, and will provide the resources and knowledge he has obtained to make this happen! For this, I applaud the Author.*

In conclusion, another one of my favorite quotes in the book is something that all young people need to hear and digest in their spirit. "We all have a purpose for being here; find it and make history by giving of yourself to help someone else". This makes me shiver because we know that giving ourselves to helping others is the way God wants us to live. Keith has given his life in helping others. Even if it meant possibly losing his life for others, he has always been willing to take the chance. This is a must read.

Humbly submitted and with love,

Kelcy

Introduction

My name is Keith Davis. Today, we are living in a society of constant change. But, most of all we are living in a ball of confusion. I have always lived my life to the best of my ability and from time to time I do find it hard to maintain a proper flow. Struggling is a way of life for some folks but in order for any change to occur we have to create a better structure for more folks to survive in this ball of confusion.

Writing is a special gift. Sometimes we write because we cannot get our message across to the number of people we would like to share our thoughts with. I write because it relieves me of many thoughts that may otherwise stay inside of me. My world is simple. I like to help people. It's funny, you would think this would be an easy task. But it's not as simple as it should be.

Can we make a path to find brighter days? I don't know but it's got to be worth a try.

When we lose someone in our life that means so much to us, how do we recover from such a loss? We Don't! Because the memories of life are never lost, only the physical. We can't see our loved ones but their spirit is eternal.

To all American persons and beyond – I am proud to be a part of this society. One thing I want to make clear to you is that I don't believe we have a world as bad as we make it seem. We are sometimes brainwashed by the media that does not share the good side of the life we live. If we could change our direction and start programming "the good" the way we program "the bad", I guarantee the result will be what we looking for...the good.

You Cannot Beat Good

Share this book with others. We all need to hear the positive beat of others.

Life is Simple

The path of life is shallow. We see very little of life and we think very small overall. We as people cannot know what is ahead if we do not take a second to believe in one another. I cannot sit alone in silence trying to explain to everyone what I am trying to say, if most ears do not want to hear it anyway. I have come a long way trying to show people each day what it means to me—life in a different way. Life is here not there, it is for everyone to enjoy. Life is for those who do not fear risk, those who cannot explain how life got them the way they are. If you do not try to change your ways, you will always blame someone else. It is you...and I tell you...it is you. I know it is you; you who cries for help and never, never wants to help yourself. Every day we can start all over.

Change for Humanity

If you've been blessed and empowered to make a change for humanity and you don't, then who are you to sit at the door of judgment when faced with injustice? At what point in life does one believe that he or she can make a difference? At what point in life does one believe in his or her duty to make a difference? At what point in life does one believe in his or her duty to humanity? At what point is one life worth more than many? The point is that when one person makes a sacrifice, at that time you are not one; you represent many. Now that's what you call honorable. Justice for all, through us we can make it happen.

Winning Spirit Award

*To every person in the
world, my gift to you.*

- *A person who gives of themselves individually to help his fellow man;*
- *A person who understands the importance of working as a team to achieve a mutual goal;*
- *A person who is passionate about his beliefs and who will persevere until his highest goals are realized;*
- *A person who recognizes that preparation is of paramount importance in overcoming adversity;*
- *A person who knows that one person can make a difference and that one person can be you;*
- *A person who recognizes all men and women as equals, deserving of opportunity and being capable of great achievement; and*
- *A person who knows that winning without honor is not winning, and winning with honor is everything.*

How ugly was the race for the president of our country, the USA? Both the Democratic and Republican nominees are full of hate and fuel their campaign with racist and bigotry expletives. Who are these future leaders teaching our kids how to hate? It is the middle of September 2016 and the tone of our future leadership is not one of concern for the growth and health of the economy. How do we stop our US companies from subbing and manufacturing their USA companies out of the USA. We have all the land we need to produce in the USA. If we are called on as the world police and are spending our resources to combat wars abroad, why can't we do both take care of our own people and also help others? It is the taxpayer's money that is being used save other lives around the world. That's okay when you have taken care of our own as well.

"Zero tolerance is unacceptable. Give a second chance. We all need a do over."

"Quotes are meant to say, what does it mean to you?"

"I can't be you but you can be yourself."

"My son says one man or woman does not make a team.
My response was one man can make a team great."

"Great minds of our time have never been wasted.
Some overlooked, some misunderstood, some not heard, some got lost."

"I have always given of myself to help others. What have you done? I hope the same."

"Give back—it's a small price we have to pay."

"If you don't believe anything I say, I wonder why I keep talking to you."

"Getting started is half of the game. The other half is finishing."

"If you want less controversy stay away from people that do not like the way you think."

"Your kids always need your love."

"Although you may not like it learn to live with it."

"It takes a minute to screw up. It takes a lifetime to repair."

"Don't be a friend today and an enemy tomorrow."

"Gift of life is what God gave you. All other gifts come from those that love you."

"Others are watching what you do."

"Really, do you want the whole world to know what you're doing?"

"Don't forget there are cameras always looking at you."

"Your where about is always known when you carry your cell phone."

"How can you be responsible to anyone if you can't be responsible for yourself?"

"Don't do something illegal and put it on the internet and be surprised when the police come to your door to arrest you."

"If you want change you may have to be the one to make that change."

"You can't say you want it and don't do what it takes to get it."

"If a car is old after one year and you assemble a new car the next year, why is it taking so long to bring new development to improve our run down inter-cities that need a new look to improve the quality of life of others? Take the old and make it new again."

"Where haven't you been that you would like to go?"

"Why do we spend so much time out of our life hating the color of someone else's skin?"

"What gives you the right to have an opinion of me when you don't even know me?"

"Spend less time talking about what you don't have and more time spending on what you want."

"We all have somewhere to go. Get there before it's too late."

"You sentence me to 150 years. How long do you expect me to live?"

"You always say you're going to go the distance but for some reason you never enter the race."

"What is rare? Seeing a space ship land on your front lawn?"

"What's funny? Sitting around with friends laughing and telling each other jokes."

"It's the 21st century. How long is it going to take to get over our prejudice and begin to think about humanity and put the hatred to bed? It's time to wake up everybody and love one another."

"Why do we have to secure each other from each other? That's a very stupid way to live life."

"As a human race overall we have become very selfish.
God's gift is wasted if we don't help to mend the problems we face in this world today."

"To conquer the impossible is to believe in yourself."

"Making your dreams come true should be important to you."

"Protect my heart–that's all I ask of you."

"If I tell you the truth and you say it's a lie, am I to believe you or myself?"

"Always strive for greatness."

"You can't stop me from being Great!"

"If you show me the way I will follow you."

"Never lose faith in yourself."

"A creative mind does not sit still. When faced with obstacles, the creative mind finds a way around…over, or whatever it takes to continue to pursue excellence. Creativity cannot be stopped!"

"Being truthful is not a lie."

"I am learning how to be with you not without you."

"Everyone is important. How important are you?"

"We are lost when we cannot find the words to express our feelings out loud."

"We all have a purpose for being here. Find it and make history by giving of yourself to help someone else."

"Walking into the light will not blind you, but seeing is believing in God taking you where light does not matter."

"We all have a gift. Using it is up to us."

"Giving back is easy, but overall we give very little of what we have as people."

"Giving will never be enough for those who think you owe them more."

"What is the world coming to? Everyone wants to blame someone else for their faults."

"*The job was not the problem. You were the problem for the job.*"

"*If I said I heard what you said and I didn't agree, that doesn't mean that I didn't understand what you said.*"

"*History is supposed to be an account of accurate events. I grew up learning that Christopher Columbus discovered America. But what's wrong is that there were already people here. Today we celebrate a holiday for this untruth.*"

"*Why do we have to try so hard to do the right thing, when we already know right from wrong?*"

"Do not try to make me see what makes sense to you when it does not make sense to me."

"A time capsule – a moment in time."

"There is no replacement for human caring and kindness."

"The beauty of life is seeing dreams come true."

"Life is worth living if you know how to live your life."

"The human race means all people, not one race of people."

"Prejudice is ignorant human insecurity, but you already know that."

"Knowing who you are is not your problem. Trying to find out who you are going to be may be your problem."

"Communication is your problem when you do not take responsibility for your actions."

"Risk is for those who do not fear losing."

"Take a chance. You will never know the outcome if you don't."

"Equality will never happen on earth. Learning to live together on earth is the goal and challenge I hope we all seek in our hearts."

"Are you old enough to not worry about what others may think of your decisions in light of the odds? Can you paint yourself with your own thoughts or do you have to use someone else's thoughts in fear of being yourself? At the end of the day you can't be anyone else other than who you are. Believe in yourself."

"Difficult times test our ability to stay strong. Even when the shadows are dark doesn't mean it's over. It just means that a change is coming for us all. Just be patient, pray, and wait. Then a change will come for all of us who believe in God. He will change it for us."

"One beat, one sound, one goal, one team; all for one another and not for any personal gain. We all have experienced hard times before, but the struggle today is the essence of tomorrow's gain."

"A lie can never be the truth."

"It is our journey. It is our time. It is our place on earth to make it better. I know not any other way to spell "giving". Give and keep giving until it becomes a habit."

"Can you imagine yourself without someone to love? When we wake up every day, we hope for many smiles in everyone's face; Jesus is all we need to get by in this world today."

"Life–a shadow of doubt with possibilities."

"Wishful thinking. Reality is life's blessing."

"You may hold me up but you will never hold me down."

"Pick up where you left off and begin again."

"Our parents want us to be what they wanted to be.
It's not our responsibility to make their failed dreams come true."

"To be successful takes practice."

"Winning is an extraordinary chance to excel."

"Stop living for the future when we already know tomorrow is not promised."

"Take a stand when you feel a need to."

"How can we explain what we do not know?"

"What is the right time and when is the right time wrong?"

"Man will always try to keep people under control and rule by fear."

"You cannot have one without the other. Or can you?"

"What is it that you want out of life that you cannot have?"

"I have never lied to anyone who did not deserve to be lied to."

"Quitting is showing your true colors."

"Why is it taking us so long to correct our own flawed system?"

"What are we really willing to do to make the world a better place?"

"Is the light at the end of the tunnel any brighter than the light you cannot see?"

"Every person has done something that makes life different today."

"Every person should have a cause."

"How long does it take to count all your blessings? You will never know."

"How long does it take to realize your own importance, and when will you decide what is important?"

"Do you have the right mate at home?"

"How can we ever measure up to ourselves?"

"An insanity plea is a loser not taking responsibility for his or her actions."

"Death is the ultimate solution for pedophiles."

"What are you willing to do to help someone else?"

"Is time the problem? What time is it and how much time do you need?"

"If we all have a brain, then why do we all not use it?"

"Find your way because it is the only way."

"Be yourself. If you don't, no one else will."

"Do you have what it takes for you to win? If so, do you know how to win?"

"Time doesn't lapse, people lapse in time."

"In time, we will find the answer to all that matters."

"The profession that kills most great men – helping others."

"When you can't get help turn to God."

"A baby's cry is saying I love you."

"What do you think? Are we all alone on this planet?"

"We can all find a new horizon, new heights to reach for if we can give something today that we would have given yesterday. If we all give more time of ourselves to help someone else, then under God we will truly see the words that are preached, that through the Lord Jesus Christ all things are possible. Thank you for sharing."

"A friend that lasts forever is one who mirrors dedication to friendship."

"Stay grounded to enjoy life."

"If we are surrounded by people, why do we really have so few true friends?"

"Approach your life and decision-making carefully, the way you would when you cross an intersection."

"*Patience is one of the components of success and fulfilling one's destiny.*"

"*Try to see someone for who they really are without prejudice and you may have a better understanding of who you really are.*"

"*How can anyone travel around the world if no one knows where it truly ends?*"

"*Is it that hard to see me?*"

"When the game is over, why is it that we then know what to do?"

"Why is it that when it is too late that we then have the answer?"

"Who owes you? Find them and get paid."

"If there is light at the end of the tunnel, then where are you?"

"Scary is sleeping under a bridge in the cold in today's society and knowing that it is home."

"Everyone has a story and a voice that wants to be heard."

"Do you ever wonder who is really listening when you complain?"

"It is never too late to find your way."

"If you do not see yourself as more, you will be less."

"Christ is our Savior, but we all knew that."

"Ask someone today how much they care about you."

"You say you love me but my question was, are you in love with me?"

"I may not listen all the time but I will listen to what I want to."

"If the dog believes he can fight, then you can say it's the fight in the dog."

"Some things are unbelievable, so don't be surprised when they cross your path."

"Don't live in fear. Look over your shoulder. Look both ways and then keep moving. Safety 101. It works."

"Approximately 70 percent of all robberies happen when you are not paying attention."

"What is real is how you feel."

"Black or white, brown or yellow, small or large, religion or gender, day or night...is all God."

"Heaven and earth is all that we know."

"Trying to be human and good to others today is a lot of work."

"We don't have to live in fear of one another."

"A whipping is okay, a beating hurts."

"You cannot be a winner unless everyone has the same opportunity."

"God gives us blessings every day."

"A one-liner is all you need if it works."

"If you get lost, remember you can come back and find yourself."

"When we were kids it was easy, so why is it so hard as adults?"

"For sure God makes a way for you and for sure He's always there. He has all you need to make it through. Thank you God."

"I pray today for hope that mankind will find a way to live in peace. I pray that all human life will give a hand to another. I pray. Pray with me."

"Life is a reunion of family and friends."

"Looking at life through only yourself gives you news of yesterday; but looking at life through others is a ball forever turning around the world for us all to learn more tomorrow."

"We all have a debt that we cannot pay; our debt is life…a note secured by God given by Him and protected by Him."

"What is giving if you wait for a return on your gift, and how are you going to be blessed if you don't understand your blessing."

"Only if you live long enough you can appreciate what you have. As we grow we will also know a friend in need is a friend indeed."

"I can't be all of this but for sure I am all of that."

"It's a shame when someone tells you what you saw when you didn't see that at all."

"Most people do not have patience because of their greed of wanting it now."

"When you are born you are in debt to God. Leave His place better than it was when you got here."

"There is one thing we do not have a clue on, and that is when life will come and when life will go."

"Why we are fighting each other today doesn't make sense."

"Common sense is easy; telling someone that it doesn't make sense at all is a challenge in itself."

"A person of color is not wrong. A group of people or persons that oppress color is wrong."

"Take a step back and think about how you really think."

"A royal flush is the truth. Nothing trumps the truth."

"Are you lonely or just stupid?"

"Drugs are not your problem. You are the problem. Drugs are the pleasure."

"It is time for all of us to set aside our petty differences.
It is time now to embrace a new way.
It is time now for us to start thinking outside the box."

"In due time we will all sacrifice enough."

"Addiction is a problem, but the problem is in you."

"Addiction is not your killer. What you are holding inside and can't let go of, is the killer. The pain and suffering you are going through will kill you if you don't let go."

"We all have a fight finish. Are you willing to continue the fight?"

"Owning a product makes sense. Owning a human being does not."

"One person's fight for injustice is a fight for humanity."

"I cannot sit by the door and protect you if you are lying to me."

"One lie leads to another, and when it starts the only solution is the truth."

"Freedom is one step from everyone's dream."

"History has shown us that being patient is all we can do."

"It's something you build slowly over time; if you work hard enough and if you respect it; it's a powerful thing called trust."

"Sometimes it's so hard to face the truth so we run."

"The beauty of our courts is that they are supposed to not judge without proper evidence."

"One cannot know what he or she doesn't study. Well, I have studied wrong and right, and I've come to the conclusion that you cannot make wrong right."

"Wanting to win and preparing to win! Where are you today when you approach the games you play?"

"You can't lose a game that is still being played."

"Money can lead to bad decisions."

"We all want to get ahead. When you get there will it be a dream come true?"

"Having more is believing in yourself. Having less is not trusting in yourself. We can all conquer success."

"Don't hold back on your dreams. They can come true, even with obstacles. You must find a way to overcome. Dreams do come true."

"It's never too late to make sacrifices. Risk is what builds a strong foundation for success."

"Respect your parents. Learn to live with who they are because they are who they are, and you can't change them. So accept them for what and who they are. Even when you disagree they will still be your parents and will always love you unconditionally."

"There is no greater sacrifice made than the one to save a human life."

"Without a doubt, from an early age we always know what's fair. If you reach out to any person or entity to ask for fairness and the day comes when your request is answered with fairness; there is only one response you can make... say "thank you". A fair response to your request has no adjustment...can't be changed. Fairness is not a compromise."

"Fairness does not have two sides. It can only be one side...fairness...period."

One Bright Moment

"The most beautiful sight in the world is when people come together and make decisions, not on their own, but collectively.
When can you make a difference? When you decide to–not a single day before."

"In time we will all see a reason. We don't know why, but there is a life-lesson to be learned from everyone."

"Why do we pray for help and then when help comes, it is not what we want."

"Time passes and we let it get away, but we know it will never stop."

"Life is not always through you, but life comes through God and God sends you angels to comfort you and you don't know who they are."

"Can you see past yourself to see someone else?"

"What's your plan? Make a plan even if you don't want to."

"The light at the end of the tunnel is where we all will go when we begin to see and have understanding."

"People hurt people and move on—it's a fact. It's wrong!!"

"I don't know if anyone really cares."

"If it doesn't matter then who cares?"

"The Blind Side is us as humans."

"If the baggage that you carry with you is toxic to others, leave it at home."

"One day you are with us, other days you are not.

Some of us live in a glass house and think that no one can throw a rock.

We're always waiting for others to do a job we can do ourselves."

"Life is a present from God. It is a gift to be packaged, stamped, and shipped "fragile." We want to always pray and ask Him to show us the way. He does this every day. He does this for you and me. How can your heart beat without Him in your life? What do you owe God?"

"Life is your debt to Him to enjoy and give to others. Only you can help Him guide you. Only you can help Him help you. He has a lot to care for. Do your part and we all can be together."

"A civil case is a civil war all over again."

"I am who I say I am. Are you?"

"Don't steal."

"There is never a wrong time to make a right decision."

"Don't let the world change your mind. Be for real."

"The negative wins when we give in and then we fail the test. Don't allow negative to win."

"I want to make sure I am right before I make a move on you."

"God will always help us.
How long do you fight before you give up? God knows your struggle and pain make no mistake. He will not allow you to give up on yourself. The Almighty, our Heaven and Earth, and our Lord Jesus Christ got your back."

"He will always help you. God is here and there and for our sake, He's everywhere. Bring Him back to you. If you haven't praised His name lately, it's time to do so. How can you control a great mind? You can't."

"Where did the old days go?"

"Being what you want to be is better than someone telling you who they want you to be."

"Interpretations of someone's intentions is a judgment of errors filled with doubt. Without prudent evidence no one can interpret anyone's intentions."

"Make life the best."

"Be you, see more, and the time has come for you to realize who you are."

"Don't let anyone take away from you who you are."

"Do not run around the problem–get rid of it."

"The longer you stay with the pain the more pain you will feel."

"I can tell you what to do, but if you don't hear me...well then...it really doesn't matter."

"If you've got everything what more do you want?"

"Humor is life's expression of how we feel."

"If you cannot feel anyone else's pain how do you expect someone to feel yours?"

"We all suffer from depression at some point in our lives."

"Why should you have to fight for what's yours? Maybe because someone is always trying to take it away."

"You can never pay back the life you have taken away."

"A smile is a smile for us all to refresh ourselves with."

"A surprise is just what it is...a surprise."

"Getting caught in a lie is just a matter of time."

"There is no one like you."

"Trust everyone and then find out if you can trust. Don't be foolish; earning trust is a setup on yourself."

"I have a lot on my plate and I cannot play cat and mouse games, but it's important that I let you know where I stand. I stand for us—period."

"I am and will always be a student of life, and being that student I have always reached for the stars."

"If you are in a position to fight injustice and you don't, then who would you become and what position would you expect others to take when they are faced with such a dilemma?"

"I've learned that to ignore the facts does not change the facts."

"I can't be anyone else but I can be me."

"One day we will come together to bring peace to God's world."

"I struggle with the truth today. No one wants to hear the truth. Why not?"

"Can I give you a loan? Can you pay me back?"

"If you build it, it will grow."

"Texting is a lack of communication."

"If you are better off without me then leave me alone."

"Brainwashing is when a leader manipulates his power to do wrong."

"Every day, as they say, is a window of opportunity. When it comes will you be ready? The true answer is that it comes every day...what's your problem? It came your way."

"The final call is when God calls you home."

"We all have a brain but few of us use it."

"Change is in all of us. We are never too old to change."

"Giving in means giving up."

"We all are loved by somebody."

"The taste of winning tastes so good."

"If you have all the answers to the questions, then tell me what's the problem?"

"Don't blame everyone else for the bad decisions you made."

"Can you change your thinking to build a common ground?"

"My legacy is my worth. I have worked hard over my lifetime to create a foundation based on trust and integrity."

"I was born to help. What about you?"

*"Do you know the outcome of not trying?
Nothing, you never tried."*

*"Say goodnight and believe that
tomorrow will come.
I'll be there for you. Will you be there for
me?"*

*"Give me a chance to let you know that
I am here for you and not for myself."*

*"I'm not here to judge you. I am here to
help you see it for yourself."*

"If I give up what I believe in then I will fall to pressure like you are saying you are doing."

"Dot your "I's" and cross the "T" in the middle and you will have Christ with you all the time."

"Always remember to cross your "T" in the middle. Christ forever."

"Common sense leads to what makes sense."

"We all have common sense. We say we don't because the more shallow we are limits that common sense."

"Are you so adamant about being right that you can't ever see yourself as wrong?"

"Who do you think you are that you can just disrespect me?"

"The dark is where you kept me. I overcame your bondage. Now I see the light and I must now move on, for there are brighter days ahead of me."

"Tell me the truth and let me deal with the outcome."

"Always pay attention to the Number 4."

"Count your blessings but never forget God sent them to you."

"Refresh your day by making someone else's day brighter."

"The power of one can serve a society for a very long time."

"No matter how old you get you can get confused."

"You gave me freedom but every day I fight for what you said you gave me."

"A gift is not a gift if someone still controls a piece of it."

"We may be ignorant but we are not stupid."

"You can't buy peace; you have to make peace."

"It's a sad day when you cannot walk down your own street."

"Building a community without leadership...think about the outcome."

"Ordering a threat on a living life is wrong."

"Would you want an assassination on your life made by someone joking or otherwise?"

"Thinking requires more than you think."

"Make a promise to yourself that you will do better."

"The holidays are not the only time you should have feelings of goodwill and of helping your fellow man. Try this task all year long."

"If you continue to hit me one day I will hit you back."

"Retaliation is a fool's way of saying I didn't forget."

"Be your best and anyone who doubts that it's your best is not for you to be around."

"The question of the day?"

"Can you measure the difference or do you need someone to do it for you?"

"Thinking of number one has no doubt of being number two."

"If you have the foresight, number one should be your goal every time."

"Being yourself is always a good way to be."

"A second chance is not for everyone."

"Living souls who are lost are mostly born from a society that represents segregation of haves and haves not."

"Talk to everyone. Someone will listen."

"Take a second to look around you before you make your next move."

"How much of what you have do you really give to help someone else?"

"Remember the air that we breathe gives us life, and is for all of us to breathe."

"Thinking less of myself is an advantage for you."

"If you know nothing you can't make sense of something."

"Is being poor worse than being broke? I wouldn't know. I am neither."

"2014 Song of the Year is "Happy". That just goes to show that we are hungry and in search of happiness."

"Competition is something you rise to, not fear."

"The other side is always wrong when the other side is right."

"No one can be independent. God made it so we will always need someone's help."

"You did not provide life for yourself. Life was given to you."

"The phrase "independent" was not for the use of being selfish. Needing no one else has to be a lonely place."

"Think of a world that only you are in. Independent of everyone else. Just you!! No fun."

"As you move forward in life, try not to believe that every human being is a reflection of the wrong another human has done to them."

"Do not compromise your integrity."

"I want my legacy to be exactly as I am... my goodwill to help others."

"I pray for all of us to love each other. What do you pray for?"

"How long have you been one dollar away from winning the lottery?"

"We all want more but we sacrifice little to obtain it."

"How does anyone know when they have given enough? You will never know."

"Success is up for us all. How many of us want to reach up?"

"Never give up on what you believe."

"Being the best is one's perfection of one's craft."

"I am not looking for a win. I am looking for justice."

"No one is too busy for you. People do what they want to do with their time."

"Do something for yourself today."

"Did you know if you don't give up, you won't give up on yourself?"

"If you're so sure that God did not give you your life, can you tell me who did?"

"Be responsible to yourself, then your responsibilities will rise to another level."

"Any party that is not for all the people is a party that is on its way to a lonely place in the corner of ignorance. They all will fall in time."

"The strength of any nation is the people who live in it."

"We cannot continue to separate ourselves from one another as people."

"What's your problem? Why can't you help someone else?"

"Your status reflects your presence."

"You are just as important as the next person."

"I leave you with this thought. What will you do to make this world a better place? We can't afford not to do our part. Love and be sincere. We all need each other."

"If you can make this world a better place, do it."

"A challenge is an obstacle to test your ability to be more than you are doing today to overcome odds stacked against you."

"God's blessing is life."

"No one person can stop you. It is your ability to stay focused which prevents your vision from being impaired by a negative force."

"Cruel and unusual punishment is letting a person sit on death row waiting to die every day."

"What is wrong with you?"

"We spend a lot of time worrying about things that never happen. Use the energy to create the things that you do want to happen."

"No one will ever understand another's plight without truly having a heart with which to feel and an ear to listen."

"Keep it simple."

"Where is nowhere?"

"You cannot lose anything that is yours."

"If I cannot reach you, then you are not reachable."

"If you get rid of a problem, have you actually fixed it?"

"First is always better than second."

"*The best thing is to not let the best thing get away.*"

"*When you have no fear, you cannot be beaten.*"

"*Do you think if you had help, you would be better off than taking advantage of the help you provide for yourself?*"

"*In today's society, money represents the high road.*"

"The skies are blue, the sun is yellow, the water is blue. What color are you?"

"To recognize skin color as a means of determining competence is a sign of ignorance."

"What color do you have to be in order to be free of prejudice?"

"Slavery is sometimes saying "I DO!!!" What happened to the word "honor"? What happened to the word "friend"? What happened to the word "trust"? What happened to the word "loyalty"? Could it be the answers lie in the soul of all of us but we do not visit our soul very often?"

"You can never fail when you're helping people."

"I know we are on our way to glory. Please fight for humanity as we move forward."

*"How do you judge me?
Do you know me at all? The spirit in
me?"*

"Why do I have to lie to you?"

*"Somebody help me. Where do I go from
here?"*

"What do you really want from me?"

*"Don't hurt me because you think you
can."*

"My actions are who I am. Really I am not you. I am who I am. Who are you?"

"The vision of one man or woman."

"Do you believe in your destiny?"

"Making the right choice can be hard sometimes."

"Patience."

"Any problem you have will have a solution. Find it and move on."

"We are all afraid of something."

"Never forget God and the Lord Jesus Christ."

"Love and happiness is the balance you need to see you through life's changes."

"Be good to all people and do not let your ignorance cloud your reason for being here."

"People are good. Media makes you think otherwise."

"Try something new and see the outcome."

"Can you imagine yourself without a friend with whom you can talk to?"

"Do not let money allow you to have vision."

"Play your cards and wait for the outcome."

"*Pick up where you left off and see if it may work somewhere else.*"

"*Leave nothing behind and then you will not ever have to remember what you forgot.*"

"*I gave you everything. And what have you given me?*"

"*Give me time. I will work it out.*"

"*Let me tell you what you don't know.*"

"*Being yourself is easy. Being someone else is hard.*"

"*Over time, the truth will prevail.*"

"*To pray for someone, you must first learn how to pray.*"

"*No one has the answer to every question.*"

"*Make it easy but make it fun.*"

"There is no equal opportunity. Equality for all will never exist."

"One life to live is what we have. Two lives are too much to handle."

"Money doesn't create power. Power lies in your resources."

"Risk has always been risky."

"It means a lot to me that you understand me."

"You can only see what you are willing to see."

"The sacrifice you give may never be enough for the sacrifices that have been given to you."

"If someone is not in your life, well, they are not supposed to be there. You think!"

"If you have lived past the age of 50, what do you know now and how are you going to live out the rest of your life?"

"I know the past is history. I know the future is what we all may search for. Honor, loyalty and morals are what make today, yesterday and tomorrow."

"Are we time sensitive?"

"Who are you?
What are you, as one, willing to do when the world needs you and your life needs to be sacrificed?"

"Mystery is a miracle waiting to happen."

"If I knew you couldn't handle it, then why did I ask you to help me? I don't know."

"What is one thing you would change in your life if you could?"

"Big things are easy to come by, but it is the small details that matter."

"You are generally right about everything you believe."

"You cannot grow if you do not want more in life."

"Try thinking of someone else before thinking of yourself."

"A big mistake will always be remembered, so try to make very few."

"Everything always works out for the good."

"Life is God's way of saying "I am here.""

"You never have to answer the unknown. You can only answer what you can."

"What debt we owe cannot ever be repaid. What life we are given cannot ever be repaid. What blessings we have cannot ever be repaid."

"If the good die young, then why are the rest of us all here?"

"The people on earth measure profit based on square footage. Based on this scenario, think about it. What are you doing with your square footage?"

"One man may cause the death of many, but there is no greater power than the one man who can save the life of many."

"Who is the victim? We will never know."

"Love is painful. Staying in love when pain exists is not love but insanity."

"Can anyone predict the end of our time? Only God knows since He created the beginning and the end."

"Your situation is no worse than anyone else's except you show it and others do not."

"Overall, we make rules to control the many not the few."

"If you stay quiet, no one will ever hear you."

"Insecurity is one person's fear."

"The Bible tells you so, but in the end you will never know until God says so."

"If you put yourself in harm's way, then do not complain about the outcome."

"Men may do a lot, but in the end man has no original ideas. Or should I say, without God no ideas exist."

"The shadow of doubt is held in the mind of those who do not believe."

"Where do you go next after you have traveled around the world?"

"I fight for life ahead. What do you fight for?"

"If not now, then when?"

"Who said what, why, how, no, yes and all of the above? All of us."

"Love is a place in our heart that keeps all of us honest emotionally."

"Avoid hurting others at all costs and enjoy the reciprocation of happiness."

"How much time do we really have when we know daily God is calling us home?"

"The sound of music is a reflection of our soul."

"Hold your hand away from your body and see who needs a helping hand."

"Everyone is looking for happiness but very few find it."

"Make no mistake, we all have a purpose for being here."

"Look at yourself. Have you lost more than you have won?"

"Be careful whom you hurt. You may find that you are also hurting yourself."

"Most people never see the light at the end of the tunnel. Why? People see very little when all they have to do is take a chance to see more. Then the light at the end of the tunnel will not blind them."

"Making less is not an issue. Why you should be making more is the issue."

"Give back what you have been given."

"As humans, we all have a piece of the world. What are you going to do with your piece?"

"One thing for sure, you cannot find a heart in the lost and found."

"A heart is in us to pump blood. What does your heart pump? KOOL AID? Cherry?"

"I thought the terminology "caged animals" was exclusive to animals but today it is reserved for humans as well."

"If I tell you that you do not know me, do not tell me that you do."

"When is it too late to do the right thing? Never."

"What are we willing to do to make the world a better place?"

"If we already know the government does not have a clue, then why do we continue to complain?"

"It brings tears to my eyes when I see homeless people mounting by the thousands from city to city and state to state, and no one is lending the right hand to bring this problem under control."

"I may not judge you. Can you judge yourself? Can you make yourself accountable?"

"Accept life as a blessing and everything else will be okay. Life will always be yours."

"Why are we here on this earth and what is it that we can't have if we really want it?"

"Dark days are the light that we are not willing to see."

"*I cannot make you see what you cannot.*"

"*Are you incapable of finding the answer for yourself?*"

"*Do you even give a damn?*"

"*Do you care about your gifts?*"

"*With all the time we are given, we still feel like we are running out of time.*"

"Why live for today when tomorrow will come?"

"Tomorrow is not promised, and it can also be said that the next second is not promised."

"You left me in the cold without a coat to keep me warm."

""Lonely at the top" is the many years of building success. So whom do you talk to when you have a problem?"

"My journey, so far, is only the distance I have traveled, but I have more distance to travel to go far into a world of the unknown."

"How many doors do you need to open before you walk through?"

"Watch your back because there is always someone who wants to climb on."

"I know there is something else we all want, but very few know exactly what that is."

"Man will always try to keep people under control and rule by fear."

"Understand the importance of what is important and separate your wishes from reality."

"How does one define rare? Rarity is a state in life in which one will never see and understand."

"Even a single life is one we need to save, for that life is our responsibility."

"*The light you are given is for others to shine through.*"

"*How can we explain what we do not know?*
Can we quit wasting our time seeing nothing and spend more time seeing something?"

"*How much time do you have to waste?*"

"*If given an opportunity to be more, would you take it? Why?*"

"Making money is not a measure of who you are."

"Why can't being happy be enough?"

"You are your worst enemy. Make friends with yourself and then you will see a change in your life."

"Am I difficult or is it your inability to hear me?"

"We cannot pick our parents. God gives us life and we hope our life is embraced by parents who are there to love and care for us."

"God created a good world for us and He wants us to take care of it."

"We are better than we know."

"Justice is not the law. Justice is men and women knowing how to do the right thing. It is taking a stand without the pressure of your peers when you know the truth."

"By giving of ourselves to charity, we make our time on earth count."

"Can we learn to give? Give Plenty. Give Always. Remember to give and make giving a habit."

"You are generally right about everything you believe."

"Striving for perfection is different from being perfect."

"*A problem big or small is still a problem.*"

"*The best I can give you is myself; nothing more or less...just myself.*"

"*Why do I have to keep explaining myself over and over again? Didn't you hear me the first time?*"

"*Grow older to see more, then you will never see less.*"

"It's in all of us to take the time out of our day to make this world a better place."

"It's not getting along that is the problem; fearing each other is the problem."

"Help change our laws to fit our times."

"If you are that smart then why do you choose to make yourself look stupid?"

"Heaven and Earth are the Eyes of Sight."

"Justice is not honorable if it's not for all."

"Terrorism is terrorism."

God is God.

Religion is our God.

Anyone who wants to put evil with God or religion as to a group of people's evil acts is wrong.

They are terrorists, period.

"Be wrong when you are wrong and just go on about your business. Get over it."

"Do not ever see yourself as being bigger than your opponent."

"Zero tolerance is humanity's stupidity. I can't make one mistake on my journey in life?"

"Forget what happened to you ten years ago so you can get on with your life."

"Can you imagine an angel in your life?"

"You have a lot. What are you going to do with it? Practice sharing."

"God is everywhere; then he's with you also. Pray for a better tomorrow and hope that today will always be yours."

"I am not your light. Your light is in you. Don't forget to turn your light on."

"In golf, there are fairways, bunkers and holes. Life has dreams, hope and blue skies."

"Your money is the same amount all over the world when you spend it."

"We all have different information."

"For one reason or another, your decision has got to make sense."

Why they call the wise man wise – My version

A wise man walked down the street and came upon a person and said, "I see that you are hungry."

"Yes," said the person.

The wise man then said, "I have a sandwich. I give you one half and I have one half." The person was outdone with thanks.

That is my version of a wise man.

"Greed is the complete opposite.
Speed and greed kill. Don't be greedy."

"If given the opportunity to do right
make that right choice."

"The outcome of nothing is nothing."

*"If you think you will lose you have lost.
If you don't think you can win you will
not.
Life is simple. People make it hard.
We all have an opinion. So what?
If you don't believe in your own ability
then who will?
Someone will thank you for your efforts,
if you deserve to be thanked."*

*"When can you make a difference? When
you decide to–not a single day before."*

Team

Team is the life that we live. We will not find anything in our lifetime that represents any one good thing outside of God, Jesus Christ, and The Holy Spirit. Team is the Dominant Force we pass in every aspect of our life. Get with it today or suffer the backlash of not being a part of the masses. There is nothing wrong with Team. Are you a team member? If not, what is your ultimate goal?

Be fearful. Be thankful. Be respectful. Be a hero. Be all you can be. Be funny. Be caught up in fun. Be all you can be. Be all of the above and more.

If I could tell the world a story, it would go like this

- *We all have so much to give to one another.*
- *Our sacrifices are without a doubt mine and yours.*
- *Without a fight, you will never know the outcome.*
- *Life is lonely when you can't find a way to enjoy it.*
- *Why must some have and others have not?*
- *How can we begin our journey without a goal?*
- *Do we all have to suffer?*
- *Why study evil when you can embrace good?*
- *God created Good.*
- *What do we really know?*
- *What will you create?*

Over Time

Over time will we know who we are?
Over time who are you to yourself?
Over time can we believe in the world itself?
Over time can love be our destiny?
Over time if we look, will we find what we are looking for?
Over time can we get along with each other?
Over time when do we know what to do?
Over time can we begin to look ahead?

Don't take life for granted. We have such a short time here.
Think about what you are doing over time.

"Have you ever been a part of something in your eyes that was a great accomplishment personally? That feeling cannot be expressed, but the joy is awesome. Try to enjoy often and not fear the unknown."

Leadership

- *Lead by example.*
- *You cannot lead if you are not willing to sacrifice the same you are asking of someone else.*
- *I am the few. The many have too many problems they don't understand.*
- *Why not be more than you expected?*
- *When will we, as people, come together to really help each other?*
- *As the world turns, where are you?*
- *I am inspired by human nature. What inspires you?*

A Message from Keith Davis

It's time to set aside our petty ways.
It's time for us to enjoy brighter days.
It's time for us to rejoice.
It's time for our families to build anew.
It's time for our families to help each other.
It's time for us to treat each other better.
It's time for us to quit pointing fingers at each other.
It's time for the young and old to quit making excuses.
It's just time for us to reach out and make a way for you and me.
That's the time I want from all of us, to quit making our problems someone else's.
Ask yourself, what time is it for you?

"The Joy of Love"

In the end, your legacy will be defined by spreading the joy of love and gift of God.

Let life give you a reason to believe we all have a purpose to give to others. We hold on so tight when we all have to give it back when we go home. What we have is not ours to keep so why hold on so tight to our treasures? So tight when we all have to give it back when we go home. Give help, show love, be kind, be human and most of all, be a person you would love and then others will enjoy you as well and love will be forever yours. The Spirit is not to be compromised.

Legacy

The times you help someone see a better way, the sacrifices you make for humanity, the times you pick up your fellow man or woman.

Your legacy will be defined by the times you didn't quit and the times that things didn't work out your way, but you found another way. Friends will be the test of who you are and when you give your word of honor make sure you know what that means; and under NO condition do you go back on your word of honor.

Leave behind a solid foundation of principles for others to follow in your footsteps.

Life...the template for it today is just as

true as yesterday. The only difference between today and yesterday is time. Your legacy for business should be not to ever compromise anything for money, no matter what your hardship may be, because that one time you do you will sell yourself forever. When you lie, cheat or steal in business, it will haunt you forever because you will always do it again. At that point you are no better than the criminal on the street. They, too, will get caught in time.

Legacy of life: if you are confused by the color of your skin or the color of your soul, the answer to your confusion is you and your faith in God and yourself. Don't live your life confused!!!

The Author of Life is God. The Gift of Life is God.
The reason for life is God and all the things we enjoy in life are not by our

will. It's God's will. Writing is not an art that belongs to us. Talent is not ours alone and as time and history pass we will learn it is great men and women like yourself that shape the foundation of life and we are not alone. We are with great company. God.

In the end, your legacy will be defined by spreading the joy of love and the gift of God.

Thank You!

I would like to thank all of my family and friends for your inspiration throughout my life.

I would like to thank my father, the Late Percy G. Davis II, my mother Irene Braswell, Sharon Davis, Wondell Collins (mother in-law). My grandparents, the Late Hosea and Elnora Davis and Sam and Sarah Nunn. Thank you to my siblings, Jesse and Patricia Smith, Percy G. Davis III, Ronald Davis, Debra Davis, Reginald Davis and Regina Davis. I would also like to thank my uncle and aunt, Robert and Bettye Davis, and special uncles and aunt the Late Michael Davis and Samuel and Odessie Williams. Thank you to my Great uncles and aunts, Eddie and Mattie Phillips, Addie Lee Phillips and the Late Rev.

Clarence Phillips and Bernice Phillips, the Late Lurean Weidman, Ethel Beason and Annie Pearl Phillips.

Thank you to my nephews and nieces, the Late Carlton Smith, Kim Smith, Jesse Smith Jr., Shanir Murrey, Trinity Smith, Jassmine Smith, Percy G. Davis IV, Laron Davis, Lucretia Charles Davis, Dalania Davis, LaTrece Davis, Robert Raddell, Sheemka Dunning, Reginald Davis Jr., and Alex Byars. And a host of great nieces and nephews.

Thank you to my cousins the Late Lucretia Quinn, Rodney and Brenda Phillips, Arthur and Shirlene Phillips, Dionne Phillips, Larry and Diane Phillips, the Late Faye Flowers, and Diane Phillips, Oliver, Anthony, Thomas, and Becky Phillips, Robert Jr. and Amy Davis, and Zuri Davis, Paul and Amber Davis-Prince, Alexis Davis,

Pam Davis, Eddie Phillips Jr., David and Pamela Phillips, Jimmie Phillips, Tyrone and Carol Bell, Charles and Jacqueline Alexander, Linda Boyd, Beverly Johnson, Larry and Calinda Collins, J.D. and Annie Boose, Samuel Bernard, Gerard and Helen Williams, Lurenda Williams Shelby, Harlan and Vanessa Fisher.

Thank you to my friends Herb Clark, Bo Rankins, Godson Bo Rankins Jr., Keith Smith, the Late John Turner, John, Kalen, and Sarah Phillips, Deloria Jones, William Jones, Arthur Jones, Eddie Newell, Kenney Newell, Mama Lena, Henry Tillman, Kenney Loman, Todd Curry, Peter Guerrero, Charlie and Dianne Joiner, Wes Chandler, Ted Hendricks, Marcus Pickett, Joe Brooks, Jaime Preciado, James Spievak, Al Van Slyke, George L. and Susanne de la Flor, Sabah Toma, Ray and Pearli Killens,

Ted Kaplan, David and Rebecca Justice, Mark Johnson, Ken Ramirez, Richard Shaw, Bruce O'Brien, Lorenzo Neal, Lem Barney, Eric Dickerson, Johnny Rodgers, Joe Greene, Rod Bernstine, Paul Warfield, Sam Seale, Sam Scarber, Calvin Sweeney, Jim Weatherley, Dave Stewart, Leo Ronces, Aleen Almoyan, Ronny Tennant, Lonnie and Linda Lucas, Nancy Newell, Eddeja Newell, Edrianna Newell, Kurt Bilben, Arely Pedroza, Darren and Vickie Carrington, and the Wells family, Mishil Yousif, Sami Harmis, Joey and Lydia Brooks, Hailey Mayer, Bonni Villalobos, Jose and Anna Belle Yap, Amber Thompson, Carlton Hill, Lonnie Butler, Reynaldo Noza.

Thank you Kadir Nelson, you have always been family and I want to thank you for allowing me to use your illustration on the front cover.

Special thank you to Jack and Ethel Martin, Lynn Phillips M.D., Vira Williams, Percy G. Davis III, Martell Goldsmith, Theodore Bates, Earnel and June Durden, Allan Durden, Karen Meints, Randy and Angela Phillips, Saad and Elizabeth Pattah, Saad Pattah Jr., Andrew Gaggo, Anthony Gaggo, Steve Caldwell, Lisette Mercado, Randy Ross, Nicholas and Clarita Aguilera, Rebecca Aguilera, and Betty Aguilera.

Thank you the greatest Etta Sunday for always being there.

Thank you Deborah Johnson as the editor.

I want to thank my cousin, Playwright/ Screenwriter Kelcy Williams for writing the foreword.

About the Author

Keith O. Davis was born and raised on the northwest side of Detroit Michigan, starting January 10, 1959. Growing up in the inner city of Detroit taught Keith at an early age how to survive. Through all the obstacles of being raised in a rough city, he overcame the struggles that came along with the challenges of being in the streets with hoodlums, versus going from elementary to high school, and getting a formal education against all odds. Early on, Keith's parents gave him the structure needed that helped him later on in life to not fall victim to the streets. Keith graduated from David

Mackenzie High School in Detroit in 1977, where he was recognized as an athlete and academic scholar. He received the Frank Gifford Athletic Academic Award.

Keith Davis' College years and beyond:

- *After graduating from high school, Keith went on to attend college in Iowa*

- *After leaving Iowa, Keith attended San Diego State University in 1981 where he once again played basketball.*

- *Keith coached Mt. Miguel JV basketball team in the mid 80's for a couple of years.*

- *After attending San Diego State College, Keith partnered with a real estate company in 1983 to 1990 named San Diego Realty and Rentals.*

- *In 1984, Keith proceeded along with a*

partner, and started another venture, an advertising publication which was put together by the Home of the Guiding Hands and (ARC), which helped the physically challenged and disadvantaged persons.

- *April, 1986 Keith became the founder of Skill Centers of America, a non-profit organization. The mission and goals of the organization were to help physically challenged and economically disadvantaged persons learn new skills.*

- *November, 1986 Skill Centers of America opened their first thrift store which was a 20,000 square foot facility. This was one of three stores that were opened; a second store was opened in 1990 and one in 1991. All were formed to benefit the programs of Skill Centers of America.*

- *1990 Keith went into another private venture; A Cajun restaurant called Café New Orleans.*

- *1990 Skill Centers of America hosted their first annual celebrity event, the Charlie Joiner Golf Tournament, which took place for 24 years. This event offered subsidizing pre-school kids tuition, scholarships for students that attended Skill Centers of America College and provided scholarships for high school graduates.*

- *1991 Keith founded Skills Centers of America College which was a vocational post-secondary school with diploma programs. Students were taught skills in graphics, reproduction and printing, retail merchandising, medical office, computerized accounting, computer operating, collections and office administration. The school also trained persons that received unemployment benefits into new skills with the changeover of society going from industrial society to a technology society.*

- *Approx. 1995 Skill Centers of America opened up a 72 kid child care center.*

- *1999 Skill Centers of America Child Care Center collaborated with neighbourhood house (Head Start program), that is on-going today.*

- *2002 Started a Country Western Label Shakedown Records.*

- *2001-2010 Keith Davis also managed a real estate empire, with shopping centers and office buildings located in San Diego and abroad.*

- *2005 Keith started C Global Distributors which provided pre-paid telephone card services and calling cards that would allow people to call out of the country. During the "Katrina" disaster and Iraq War, C Global provided a U.S. Patriot card that was sent to members of the Armed Forces so they could call home for free as well as Katrina victims.*

- *In approximately 2008, Keith also opened up a restaurant, "On Hit Barbeque Pit". There were locations on the naval base in San Diego called North Islands and 32nd Street, in National City location.*

- *In 2010, Keith started a-barbeque sauce company called "Real Deal Barbeque", now known as "Players Choice Barbeque Sauce".*

- *All of Keith's life he has been a Philanthropist and Humanitarian; donating his time to help out others. In 2009 he cooked 205 turkeys along with all the fixings and donated the food to Navy men and women.*

In 2007, Keith found out that there were classmates of his that did not have enough money to attend their 30 year high school reunion. Keith decided to pay for the entire reunion so that everyone could go for free. These are just some of the things Keith has done.

Keith has now wrote his first book which is a collaboration of years and years of experience.

Printed in the United States
By Bookmasters